YOU CAN TRUST GOD

by Jerry Bridges

NAVPRESS

A MINISTRY OF THE NAVIGATORS
P.O. BOX 6000, COLORADO SPRINGS, COLORADO 80934

The Navigators is an international Christian organization. Our mission is to reach, disciple, and equip people to know Christ and to make Him known through successive generations. We envision multitudes of diverse people in the United States and every other nation who have a passionate love for Christ, live a lifestyle of sharing Christ's love, and multiply spiritual laborers among those without Christ.

NavPress is the publishing ministry of The Navigators. Nav-Press publications help believers learn biblical truth and apply what they learn to their lives and ministries. Our mission is to stimulate spiritual formation among our readers.

The content of this booklet is adapted from *Trusting God* by Jerry Bridges, published by NavPress. To fully benefit from the author's message, the reader is encouraged to enjoy a complete reading of *Trusting God*, which is available through Christian book-stores.

All Scripture quotations in this publication are from the *Holy Bible: New International Version* (NIV), Copyright © 1973, 1978, 1984, International Bible Society. Used by permission of Zondervan Bible Publishers.

Printed in the United States of America

9 10 11 12 13 14 15 16 17 / 99

FOR A FREE CATALOG OF
NAVPRESS BOOKS & BIBLE STUDIES,
CALL 1-800-366-7788 (USA)
or 1-416-499-4615 (CANADA)

YOU CAN TRUST GOD

Can You Trust God?

A couple of years ago, a large malignant tumor was found in my wife's abdominal cavity. She went through radiation therapy, chemotherapy, and all of the pain, nausea, and months of anxious waiting that go along with this disease. Watching her suffer cut me to the heart as well. After many months, the Lord ended her struggle through death.

Our experience is nothing extraordinary these days. In fact, in the past few years I have had seven friends with cancer listed on my "urgent" prayer page.

But cancer or other physical ailments are not the only source of anxiety. Over lunch a few weeks ago a businessman friend confided that his company is perilously close to bankruptcy; another experiences heartache over a spiritually rebellious teenager. On a larger scale, we read in our daily newspapers of war, terrorism, earthquakes, famine, racial injustice, murder, and exploitation in various parts of the world.

The truth is, all of us face adversity in various forms. So the question naturally arises, "Where is God in all of this?" Can you really trust God when adversity strikes and fills your life with pain? Does He indeed come to the rescue of those who seek Him? Does He, as Psalm 50:15 affirms, deliver those who call upon Him in the day of trouble?

Can you trust God? The question itself has two possible meanings. Can you *trust* God, i.e., is He dependable in times of adversity? But the second meaning is also critical: Can *you* trust God? Do you have such a relationship with God and such a confidence in Him that you believe He is with you in your adversity even though you do not see any evidence of His presence and His power?

Trusting in the Unknown

It is not easy to trust God in times of adversity. No one enjoys pain, and when it comes, we want it relieved as quickly as possible. Even the Apostle Paul pleaded with God three times to take away the thorn in his flesh, before he finally found God's grace to be sufficient. I have been there often enough myself to know something of the distress, the despair, and the darkness that fills our souls when we wonder if God truly cares about our plight. I have spent a good portion of my adult life encouraging people to pursue holiness, to obey God. Yet, I acknowledge it often seems more difficult to trust God than to obey Him.

God's moral will, which is given to us in the Bible, is rational and reasonable. The circumstances in which we must trust God often appear irrational and inexplicable. God's law is readily recognized to be good for us, even when we don't want to obey it. The circumstances of our lives frequently appear to be dreadful and grim, or perhaps even calamitous and tragic. Obeying God is worked out within well-defined boundaries of God's revealed will. Trusting God is worked out in an arena that has no boundaries. We do not know the extent, the duration, or the frequency of the painful, adverse circumstances in which we must frequently trust God. We are always coping with the unknown.

Yet it is just as important to trust God as it is to obey Him. When we disobey God we defy His authority and despise His holiness. But when we fail to trust God we doubt His sovereignty and question His goodness. In both cases we cast aspersions upon His majesty and His character.

In order to trust God, we must always view our adverse circumstances through the eyes of faith, not of sense. And just as the faith of salvation comes through hearing the gospel (Romans 10:17), so the faith to trust God in adversity comes through the Word of God alone. It is only in Scripture that we find an adequate view of God's relationship to and involvement in our painful circumstances. It is only from the Scriptures, applied to our hearts by the Holy Spirit, that we receive the grace to trust God in our adversity.

The Scriptures teach us three essential truths about God that we must believe if we are to trust God in adversity. They are:

- God is completely sovereign.
- God is infinite in wisdom.
- God is perfect in love.

Someone has expressed these three truths as they relate to us in this way: "God, in His love, always wills what is best for us. In His wisdom, He always knows what is best, and in His sovereignty, He has the power to bring it about."

Choosing to Trust

Margaret Clarkson, in speaking of how we may begin to accept adversity in our lives, said, "Always it is initiated by an act of will on our part; we set ourselves to believe in the overruling goodness, providence, and sovereignty of God and refuse to turn aside . . . no matter how we feel."[1]

For many years in my own pilgrimage toward trusting God at all times—I am still far from the end of the journey—I was a prisoner to my feelings. I mistakenly thought I could not trust God unless I *felt* like trusting Him (which I almost never did in times of adversity). Now I am learning that trusting God is first a matter of the will, and is not dependent on my feelings. I choose to trust God and my feelings eventually follow.

But though trusting God is a matter of the will, it is first of all a matter of knowledge. We must *know* that God is sovereign, wise, and loving. Having been exposed to the knowledge of the truth, we must then choose whether to believe it or to follow our feelings. We must say to God, "I will trust You though I do not feel like doing so."

I do not mean to suggest that the choice is as easy as choosing whether or not I will go to the grocery store, or even choosing whether or not I will do some sacrificial deed. Trusting God is a matter of faith, and faith is the fruit of the Spirit (Galatians 5:22). Only the Holy Spirit can make His Word come alive in our hearts and create faith, but we can choose to look to Him to do that, or we can choose to be ruled by our feelings of anxiety or resentment or grief.

Admitting Our Helplessness

John Newton, author of the hymn "Amazing Grace," watched cancer slowly and painfully kill his wife over a period of many months. In recounting those days, Newton said,

I believe it was about two or three months before her death, when I was walking up and down the room, offering disjointed prayers from a heart torn with distress, that a thought suddenly struck me, with unusual force, to this effect— "The promises of God must be true; surely the Lord will help me, *if I am willing to be helped*!" It occurred to me, that we are often led . . . [from an undue regard of our feelings], to indulge that unprofitable grief which both our duty and our peace require us to resist to the utmost of our power. I instantly said aloud, "Lord, I am helpless indeed, in myself, but I hope I am willing, without reserve, that Thou shouldest help me."[2]

Newton was helped in a remarkable way. During those remaining months he carried out his duties as an Anglican minister and was able to say, "Through the whole of my painful trial, I attended all my stated and occasional services, as usual." He even preached his wife's funeral sermon.

How was John Newton helped? First, he chose to be helped. He realized it was his duty to resist "to the utmost of our power" an inordinate amount of grief and distraction. He realized it was sinful to wallow in self-pity. Then he turned to the Lord, not even asking, but only indicating his *willingness* to be helped. He wrote, "I was not supported by

8

lively sensible consolations, but by being able to realize to my mind some great and leading truths of the word of God."[3]

The Spirit of God helped him by making the needed truths of Scripture alive to him. He chose to trust God, he turned to God in an attitude of dependence, and he was enabled to realize certain great truths of Scripture. The crucial elements that led him to trust God were:

- choice;
- prayer;
- the Word of God.

The same David who said in Psalm 56:4, "In God I trust; I will not be afraid" said in Psalm 34:4, "I sought the LORD, and he answered me; he delivered me from all my fears." There is no conflict between saying, "I will not be afraid" and asking God to deliver us from our fears. David recognized it was his responsibility to choose to trust God, but also that he was dependent on the Lord for the ability to do it.

Whenever I teach on the subject of personal holiness, I always stress the fact that we are *responsible* to obey the will of God, but also that we are *dependent* upon the Holy Spirit for the enabling power to do it. The same principle applies in the realm of trusting God. We are responsible to trust Him in times of adversity, but we are dependent upon the Holy

Spirit to enable us to do so.

Trusting God does not mean we do not experience pain. It means we believe that God is at work through the occasion of our pain for our ultimate good. It means we work back through the Scriptures regarding His sovereignty, wisdom, and goodness and ask Him to use those Scriptures to bring peace and comfort to our hearts. It means, above all, that we do not sin against God by allowing distrustful and hard thoughts about Him to sway our minds. It will often mean that we have to say, "God, I don't understand, but I trust You."

Our Trustworthy God

The whole idea of trusting God is, of course, based upon the fact that God is absolutely trustworthy. We must be firmly grounded in the scriptural truths concerning His sovereignty, wisdom, and love if we are to trust Him. (The Bible study on pages 17-19 is a good way to start.)

We must also lay hold of some of the great promises of His constant care for us. One such promise is Hebrews 13:5: "Never will I leave you; never will I forsake you." The Puritan preacher Thomas Lye remarked that in this passage the Greek has five negatives and may thus be rendered, "I will not, not leave thee; neither will I not, not forsake thee."[4] Five times God emphasizes to us that He will not forsake us. He wants us to firmly grasp the truth that whatever circumstances may indicate, we must believe, on the basis of His promise, that He has not forsaken us or left us to the mercy of those circumstances.

We may sometimes lose the *sense* of God's presence and help but we never lose them. Job, in his distress, could not find God. He said:

> "But if I go to the east, he is not there;
>> if I go to the west, I do not find
>> him.
> When he is at work in the north, I do not
>> see him;
>> when he turns to the south, I catch
>> no glimpse of him.
> But he knows the way that I take;
>> when he has tested me, I will come
>> forth as gold." (Job 23:8-10)

Job apparently wavered, as we do, between trust and doubt. Yet here we see a strong affirmation of trust. He couldn't find God anywhere. God had completely withdrawn from Job the comforting sense of His presence. But Job believed, though he couldn't see Him, that God was watching over him, and would bring him through that trial as purified gold.

You and I will sometimes have the same experience as Job—not the same kind or intensity of sufferings, but the inability to find God anywhere. God will seem to hide Himself from us. Even the prophet Isaiah once said to

11

God, "Truly you are a God who hides himself, O God and Savior of Israel" (Isaiah 45:15). We should learn from Job and Isaiah, so that we are not totally surprised and dismayed when, in the time of our distress, we can't seem to find God. At these times we must cling to His bare but inviolate promise, "Never will I leave you; never will I forsake you."

The Apostle Paul speaks of "God, who does not lie" (Titus 1:2). This is the God who has promised, "Never will I leave you; never will I forsake you." He may hide Himself from our sense of His presence, but He never allows our adversities to hide us from Him. He may allow us to pass through the deep waters and the fire, but He will be with us in them (Isaiah 43:2).

Because God will never leave you nor forsake you, you are invited, in the words of Peter, to "cast all your anxiety on him because he cares for you" (1 Peter 5:7). God cares for you! He is not just there with you, He cares for you.

His care is constant—not occasional or sporadic. His care is total—even the very hairs of your head are numbered. His care is sovereign—nothing can touch you that He does not allow. His care is infinitely wise and good so that, again in the words of John Newton, "If it were possible for me to alter any part of his plan, I could only spoil it."[5]

We must learn to cast our anxieties on Him. So we are back to the matter of choice.

We must, by an act of the will in dependence on the Holy Spirit, say something such as, "Lord, I choose to cast off this anxiety onto You, but I cannot do this of myself. I will trust You by Your Spirit to enable me, having cast my anxiety on You, not to take it back upon myself."

Trust is not a passive state of mind. It is a vigorous act of the soul by which we choose to lay hold on the promises of God and cling to them despite the adversity that at times seeks to overwhelm us.

Sovereignty, Love, and Wisdom

So trusting God is a choice based on knowledge of Scripture and on prayer in an attitude of dependence. The first step is to approach the Bible with the desire to embrace the knowledge it offers. There are dozens of passages we could look at regarding God's sovereignty, love, and wisdom, but for now consider just a few.

> Who can speak and have it happen
>   if the Lord has not decreed it?
> Is it not from the mouth of the Most
>   High
>   that both calamities and good
>   things come?
>   (Lamentations 3:37-38)

This passage offends many people. They find it difficult to accept that both calamities and good things come from God. People often ask the question, "If God is a God of love, how could He allow such a calamity?" But Jesus Himself affirmed God's sovereignty in calamity when Pilate said to Him, "Don't you realize I have power either to free you or to crucify you?" Jesus replied, "You would have no power over me if it were not given to you from above" (John 19:10-11). Jesus acknowledged God's sovereign control over His life.

Because God's sacrifice of His Son for our sins is such an amazing act of love toward us, we tend to overlook that for Jesus it was an excruciating experience beyond all we can imagine. In His humanity it was a calamity sufficient to cause Him to pray, "My Father, if it is possible, may this cup be taken from me" (Matthew 26:39), but He did not waver in His assertion of God's sovereign control.

Rather than being offended over the Bible's assertion of God's sovereignty in both good and calamity, believers should be comforted by it. Whatever our particular calamity or adversity may be, we may be sure that our Father has a loving purpose in it. As King Hezekiah said, "Surely it was for my benefit that I suffered such anguish" (Isaiah 38:17). God does not exercise His sovereignty capriciously, but only in such a way as His infinite love deems best for us. Jeremiah wrote,

Though he brings grief, he will show
compassion,

> so great is his unfailing love.
> For he does not willingly bring affliction
> or grief to the children of men.
>
> (Lamentations 3:32-33)

Many people talk about God's providence but have only a vague idea of what it means. I define God's providence as *His constant care for and absolute rule over all His creation for His own glory and the good of His people.* Note the absolute terms: *constant* care, *absolute* rule, *all* creation. Nothing, not even the smallest virus, ecapes His care and control.

But note also the twofold objective of God's providence: His own glory and the good of His people. These two objectives are never antithetical; they are always in harmony with each other. God never pursues His own glory at the expense of His people's good, nor does He ever seek our good at the expense of His glory. He has designed His eternal purpose so that the two are inextricably bound together.

What comfort and encouragement this should be to us! If we are going to trust God in adversity, we must believe that just as certainly as God will allow nothing to subvert His glory, so He will allow nothing to spoil the good He is working out in us and for us. Is God trustworthy? The Bible is clear that He *can* always care for us (He is sovereign) and that He *does* always care for us (He is good).

But how can God care for all of us at the same time that He cares for His glory? And how

15

are tragedies consistent with such care? God's sovereignty is also exercised in infinite wisdom, far beyond our ability to comprehend. After surveying God's sovereign but inscrutable dealings with His own people, the Jews, the Apostle Paul bows before the mystery of God's actions with these words:

> Oh, the depth of the riches of the
> wisdom and knowledge of God!
> How unsearchable his judgments,
> and his paths beyond tracing out!
> (Romans 11:33)

Paul acknowledged what we must acknowledge if we are to trust God. God's plan and His ways of working out His plan are frequently beyond our ability to fathom and understand. We must learn to trust when we don't understand.

One final thought: In order to trust God, we must know Him in an intimate, personal way. David said in Psalm 9:10, "Those who know your name will trust in you, for you, LORD, have never forsaken those who seek you." To know God's name is to know Him intimately. It is more than just knowing facts about God. It is coming into a deeper personal relationship with Him as a result of seeking Him in the midst of our pain and discovering Him to be trustworthy. It is only as we know God in this personal way that we come to trust Him. As you delve into the Scriptures about

16

God's sovereignty, wisdom, and love, pray that the Holy Spirit of God will enable you to get beyond the facts about God, so that you will come to know Him better, and so be able to trust Him more completely.

Summary

God deserves your trust because He is:

- completely sovereign;
- infinite in wisdom;
- perfect in love.

It is not always easy to feel like trusting God. But trusting Him is a matter of *choosing* to trust because of what we *know*, despite what we *feel*.

God's Spirit enables us to trust Him in the midst of suffering when we:

- admit our helplessness to trust;
- choose to seek God's help to trust;
- pray for the grace to trust;
- immerse ourselves in Scriptures about God's trustworthiness;
- choose to act on what we know, rather than on what we feel.

For Reflection and Action

1. a. In what situation in your life are you currently having the most difficulty trusting God?

   b. Take time right now to tell God exactly how you are feeling about this situation. Tell Him all of your fears and hurts. Confess to Him that you are not able to make yourself trust Him about this.

When you've expressed all of your feelings to God, ask Him for the grace to trust Him despite your feelings.

2. Read Romans 8:18-39. Make a list of all the reasons for trusting God that you find in this passage.

3. What good could God possibly bring from the situation you are currently struggling with? God often doesn't show us the whole picture, but ask Him to give you some glimpses.

4. What reasons for trusting God do you find in the following passages?

   Psalm 147:5

   Isaiah 46:10

Isaiah 54:10

Matthew 10:29-31

Romans 5:6-8

For Meditation

Choose one of the passages in this booklet
that especially speaks to the reason why you
are having trouble trusting God. (Consider
those below and in question 4.) Ask God to
write the verse you choose on your heart.
Then read it aloud to yourself several times a
day until you have memorized it. Think about
how it applies to your situation.

> *Though he brings grief, he will show
> compassion,*
> *so great is his unfailing love.*
> *For he does not willingly bring affliction*
> *or grief to the children of men.*
> *(Lamentations 3:32-33)*

> *We know that in all things God works for
> the good of those who love him, who
> have been called according to his pur-*

pose. For those God foreknew he also predestined to be conformed to the likeness of his Son, that he might be the firstborn among many brothers.
(Romans 8:28-29)

Oh, the depths of the riches of the
wisdom and knowledge of
God!
How unsearchable his judgments,
and his paths beyond tracing out!
(Romans 11:33)

Notes

1. Margaret Clarkson, *Grace Grows Best in Winter* (Grand Rapids, Mich.: Eerdmans Publishing Company, 1984), page 21.

2. John Newton, *The Works of John Newton* (Edinburgh: The Banner of Truth Trust, 1985), volume 5, pages 621-622.

3. Newton, pages 623-624.

4. *Puritan Sermons 1659-1689*, a collection of sermons by seventy-five Puritan preachers, originally published at irregular intervals between 1660 and 1691, in London (Wheaton, Ill.: Richard Owens Roberts, Publisher, 1981), volume 1, page 378.

The NavPress Booklet Series includes:

A Woman of Excellence
by Cynthia Heald

Avoiding Common Financial Mistakes
by Ron Blue

Building Your Child's Self-Esteem
by Gary Smalley & John Trent

Claiming the Promise
by Doug Sparks

Dealing with Desires You Can't Control
by Mark R. McMinn

God Cares About Your Work
by Doug Sherman & William Hendricks

How to Deal with Anger
by Larry Crabb

How to Handle Stress
by Don Warrick

How to Have a Quiet Time
by Warren & Ruth Myers

**How to Keep Your Head Up
When Your Job's Got You Down**
by Doug Sherman

How to Know God's Will
by Charles Stanley

How to Overcome Loneliness
by Elisabeth Elliot

Prayer: Beholding God's Glory

When You Disagree: Resolving Marital Conflicts
by Jack & Carole Mayhall

You Can Trust God
by Jerry Bridges